PACKS
Strength in Numbers

Hannah Salyer

HOUGHTON MIFFLIN HARCOURT

Boston   New York

Packs,

herds,

huddles,

and pods.

Together,

we are better.

When we ants head underground, we are known as a *nest*. We march miles across the forest floor, gathering green leaves as we go. Once we return to our colony, we store the leaves in our cellar to help grow food that we eat later.

Together, we harvest!

In billows, we bats take to the skies, forming a *cloud*. Flitting
and flapping, yipping and yapping, we form strong bonds
with our family. We love to gab, but all that yammer is not
just chatter: it's echolocation, a series of high-pitched calls we
use to detect our prey and our surroundings.

Together, we speak!

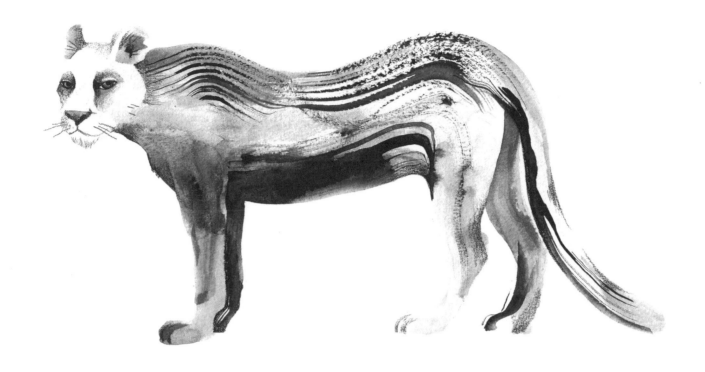

We lions live in a *pride,* and proud we are. Our strong bonds come from our keeping close: we use purrs, licks, and nuzzles to express our feelings and relate to one another.

Together, we nurture!

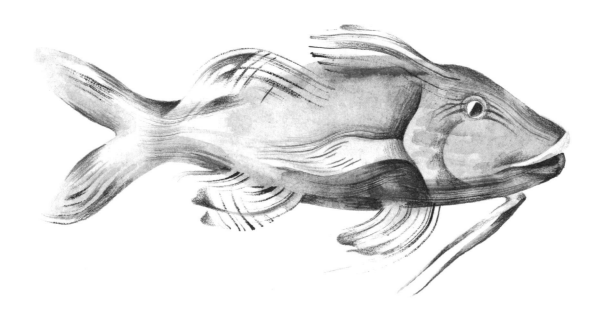

We bright yellow fish are known as a *school*. We are quite formidable as a team when we stalk the reef in a large group, chasing and circling our unsuspecting prey.

Together, we hunt!

We are wildebeest, also known as gnus, and our herd is called an *implausibility*—often a million strong. We are the largest species of antelope to roam the Serengeti. Every year we migrate and cover lots of ground; we follow the rain and use our numbers as a shield to keep predators at bay.

Together, we travel!

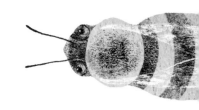

In flight, we bees are called a *swarm*. While some of us zip and buzz from blossom to blossom, others stay home to care for the young. We pollinate flowers, tend to the hive, and make delicious honey.

Together, we work!

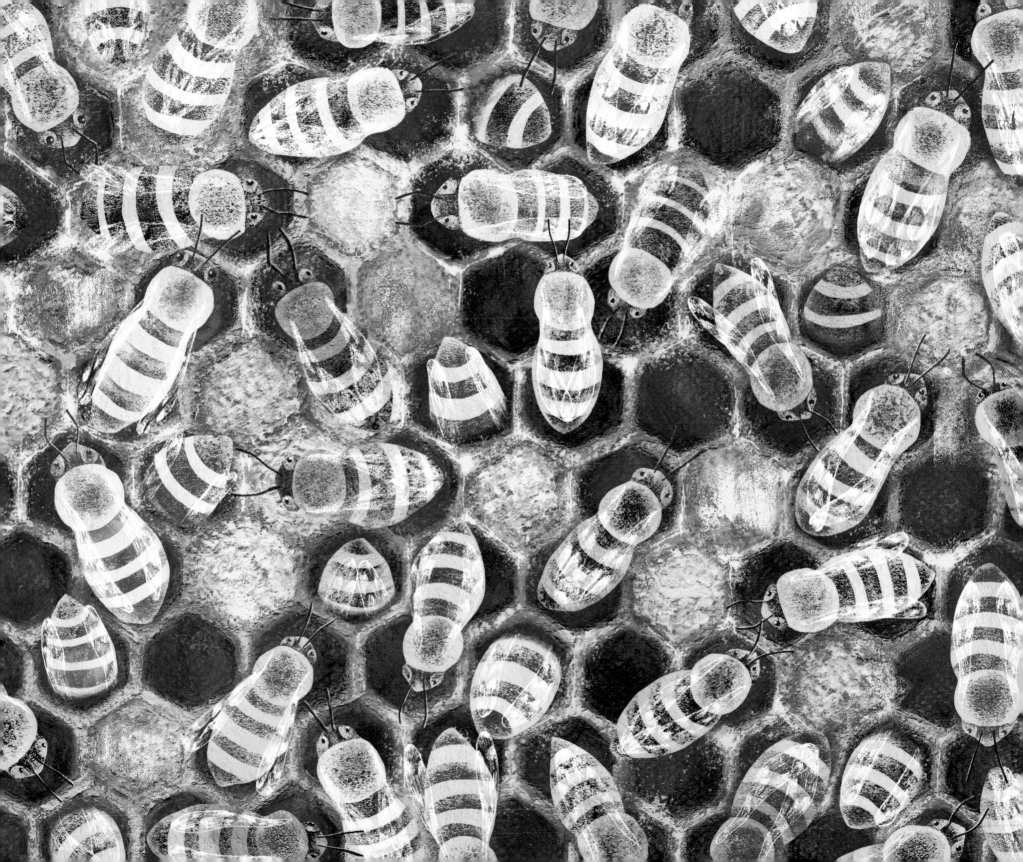

We frogs can become one noisy *army*! When the winter ice melts away, we put on a grand performance to find the perfect partners. You can hear us chirp and bellow our love songs between the tall swaying grasses of marshes, ponds, and swamps.

Together, we sing!

We are coral—that's plural to you. We exist as a *colony* and are vital beings in the fabric of the sea. As individuals, we are tiny—but when we link up, we create a large colorful reef that is home to many other ocean dwellers.

Together, we build!

Together, we confuse predators!

Many mongooses make a *mob*, but don't let our sweet looks fool you: we are sneaky and tough. At sundown we gather into a protective cluster, and, with our sleek tails curled tight, our eldest family members keep an eye out for danger.

Together, we sleep!

We flamingos can be found in the thousands! We are known as a *flamboyance*. We do everything together: feed, flock, sleep, and grow. When it's time to find our mates, we frolic in a fabulous fox trot.

Together, we dance!

Together, we bask in the sun!

All together . . .

. . . we are better!

While many creatures of all species, shapes, and sizes—human and non-human alike—flourish in packs or groups, we also don't rely solely on our own kind to survive. Big, small, two-footed, four-footed, feathered, or furry, the diversity on our planet helps us all thrive.

Sadly, many of the animals in this book are under threat from things like climate change, poaching, or habitat loss.

So what can we do? We can learn more about these animals! Read books, watch documentaries, plant a garden, and always pick up after ourselves. Research and find out more about how every type of creature has a special and important role to play on our planet—even us! Look into conservation programs that are helping protect these creatures and write letters to these organizations. Talk about them with friends and family, and make art and stories about them.

We can strive to be gentle, kind, and thoughtful to all the beings who make our world better.

1. Bottlenose dolphin
2. Greater flamingo
3. Banded mongoose
4. Southern lion
5. Mexican free-tailed bat
6. American bison

7. Spring peeper
8. American crocodile
9. Emperor penguin
10. Grevy's zebra
11. Monarch butterfly
12. Blue wildebeest

13. Western honeybee
14. Alaskan timber wolf
15. Human (you!)
16. Pillar coral
17. *Zoanthus*
18. Staghorn coral

19. Plate coral
20. Brain coral
21. Blue coral
22. *Antipathes*
23. Leaf-cutter ant
24. Goldsaddle goatfish

Further Reading

Gardner, Kate. *Lovely Beasts: The Surprising Truth*. Illustrated by Heidi Smith. New York: Balzer + Bray, 2018.

Hall, Kirsten. *The Honeybee*. Illustrated by Isabelle Arsenault. New York: Atheneum Books for Young Readers, 2018.

McAllister, Angela. *Wild World*. Illustrated by Hvass&Hannibal. New York: Wide Eyed Editions, 2018.

Messner, Kate. *The Brilliant Deep: Rebuilding the World's Coral Reefs: The Story of Ken Nedimyer and the Coral Restoration Foundation*. Illustrated by Matthew Forsythe. San Francisco: Chronicle Books, 2018.

Wenzel, Brendan. *Hello Hello*. San Francisco: Chronicle Books, 2018.

Wood, Amanda, and Mike Jolley. *Natural World: A Visual Compendium of Wonders from Nature*. Illustrated by Owen Davey. New York: Wide Eyed Editions, 2016.

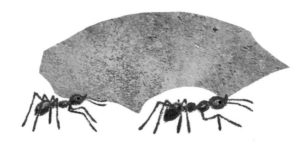

For the pack that helped me make this book;
immense gratitude to Abigail, Kirsten, Kate,
Cara, Maxim, and my mother, Tracey.

hmhbooks.com

The illustrations in this book were done in cut paper, gouache,
acrylic paint, and colored pencils and finished digitally.
The text type was set in Burin.
Book design by Cara Llewellyn

Library of Congress Cataloging-in-Publication Data

Names: Salyer, Hannah, author.
Title: Packs : strength in numbers / Hannah Salyer.
Description: Boston : Houghton Mifflin Harcourt, [2019] | Audience: Age 4–7.
| Audience: K to Grade 3. | Includes bibliographical references and index.
Identifiers: LCCN 2018052149 | ISBN 9781328577887 (hardcover picture book)
Subjects: LCSH: Social behavior in animals—Juvenile literature. | Animal
societies—Juvenile literature.
Classification: LCC QL775 .S25 2019 | DDC 591.5—dc23
LC record available at https://lccn.loc.gov/2018052149

Manufactured in Malaysia
TWP 10 9 8 7 6 5 4 3 2 1
4500777528

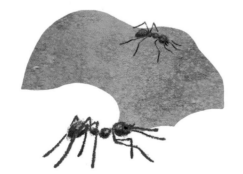